The Perfect Mindset for Success

Leaders Notebook

the growth mindset

VS

the fixed mindset

If You Want To Know How Successful Stay Successful Again & Again **This Book Is For You Then**

Leaders Notebook

there is a psychological trait, that all successful people appear to have in common it's been co-signed by **Bill Gates** and **NASA** uses it as a criteria for selecting potential systems engineers this concept is called **the growth mindset.**
 a term originally coined by **Carol Dweck** people with the growth mindset "believe that intelligence are skilled in any field can be developed through effort basically they believe that anyone can nurture their abilities"

In anything the inverse of the growth mindset is **the fixed mindset,**
people with this one believe that intelligence and skill are innate it's something that we're born with we're either: **born gifted** or **not** there's no room for change basically they believe intelligence is fixed from birth in this essay,we'll explore why the growth mindset is the better one and how we can develop it so we talked a little about what the growth mindset is the belief that intelligence

And skill in any field can be developed.
 but, let's also talk about what it's not,
it's not magic it won't help you get everything that you want out of life and it won't make you the next **Elon Musk** or **Steve Jobs**.
however, it is a very powerful lens with which to see the world and it can improve the probability of your success.
all of us are a mixture of both growth and fixed mindsets in some areas of our lives with growth mindset.

In others we operate with **the fixed mindset.**
because of this I want you to think of both mindsets like a pair of glasses some people were the growth glasses more often and others where the fixed glasses more.
 but, we all wear both in different situations in our lives.
although we
should all strive to where the growth one's much more than we wear the fixed ones but why well a lot of research seems to suggest :

that people with **the growth mindset** are <u>more successful</u> than people with the **fixed mindset**.

for example, a study found that students who held a growth mindset were three times more likely to score in the top **20%** on the test, while students with a fixed mindset were four times more likely to score in the bottom **20%.**

 another study another study found that when seventh graders participated in a **growth mindset** program

they were able to avoid a drop in grades, which usually occurs in middle school people with **the growth mindset** are much more resilient, which allows them to overcome challenging and difficult situations.
because, they prioritize learning over failure they're unafraid **to take risks** they prioritize growing over stagnation.
on the other hand, people with **the fixed mindset** don't want to challenge themselves

because, they believe talent and intelligence are fixed they look at failure as an assault on who they are as a person to them lack of knowledge is an indicator of stupidity and failure.
once means failure always a person with **the growth mindset**, believes that they're always in a state of flux and transformation so they don't attach their identity to the results. instead they focus on the process of **growing** and **learning**.

few people will deny that the **growth mindset** seems to map nicely onto reality we know that the brain can continue to learn until the day we die thanks to the field of "neuroscience".
it also seems quite intuitive that people must work hard and persevere despite obstacles to end up being successful.
so the growth mindset to be a much more accurate view of reality than the fixed mindset people with the growth mindset are living in:

greater accordance with reality, than people with **the fixed mindset** they can make truer decisions whereas a person with the fixed mindset lives in a greater state of delusion what do I mean by this:
imagine two entrepreneurs one has **the growth mindset** we said before :

"the growth mindset is the belief that intelligence and skill in any field can be developed"

and one has a **fixed mindset** there are both in the early stages of their **"entrepreneurial journey"**. suddenly, they both encounter a **roadblock** and are forced to make a decision the one with the fixed mindset sees the long and arduous journey ahead of her due to the roadblock the journey is in the way of what matters to her the result she believes that :
entrepreneurship should come easy to those who are destined for it she decides to

quit the one with **the growth mindset** sees the long and arduous journey ahead of her and smiles.

the journey is the way for her the journey is what matters taking the role of a student she accepts the long and arduous path as her teacher, she will allow it to mold her into the person, she needs to become to achieve the result she desires she decides to persist.

when we look at both of these examples most of us would agree that :

"the entrepreneur" with the growth mindset has a greater understanding of reality her decision is truer we know that things take time effort and strategy to team.

but, it's often difficult to put that kind of thinking into practice.

so how can we develop the growth mindset ?

the first key to develop a growth mindset is actually very simple understanding that :

<u>it exists and that it's possible for the brain to change</u>

neuroscience has shown that our brains are not fixed and in fact,
they're very malleable we can always grow and learn new skills.
for example, a study found that taxicab drivers develop more gray matter in their brains to help them navigate more effectively in large cities. they also found that the amount of gray matter in their brains were correlated with thenumber of years that they had been working as a taxi driver.

this suggests that the act of driving a taxi led to changes in their brains which allowed them to be more effective at their job.

the second key is to focus on process over results **Dweck** has said that "**we should praise others for their efforts in their process rather than praising them for the results**". for example, it's better to say you studied very effectively for that test and your hard work really paid off rather than you're so smart you got an **A**

in the former example, we're focusing in on and praising the students process which is something that they can control.
hopefully, they'll learn to associate themselves and their results with that process ,however, in the latter example we praised the student for a result which is ultimately out of their control.
unfortunately, this student will likely begin to associate themselves with the result.
I think it's really important to

emphasize that it's not easy to pass a growth mindset onto others it's not as simple as telling someone that they're a hard worker, and that they just need to put in the effort they need to internalize that they can change the results by changing the process so they need to know how to effectively create a process, alter it and produce results from that. my solution to this is to keep a journal pick an activity that you want to get really good at for example :

let's say that I want to get really good at math, in the journal I'll write down my process for studying mathematics, I list out the steps and put a quantifiable measurement, to as many things as I can. for example : my process might look like this review my notes once a day do 10 practice problems a day and meet with my professor for 30 minutes a week so my process has been solidified and everything has been quantified now I need to designate a result that I'm looking for I need a target to aim at.

let's say that I'm looking for a grade of 80% or higher on my next exam when I get my exam work back I compare it to my goal if it's higher than I know my system works

but, I can still go back and alter parts of it to see if I can do even better or I can try and optimize it, maybe, I can spend less time reading the textbook and more time doing practice problems if my grade comes back lower I definitely need to :

go back and refine my process.

I believe this method of keeping a journal creating a process and refining it until the desired outcome is achieved will help promote. the growth mindset it keeps our mind focused on a changeable process the results are measured and paid attention to only as an indicator of how well our process worksthe process. either works as intended or a dozen but it says nothing of the person the process is :

always malleable it's not that it doesn't work it just doesn't work yet.

I think another good idea is to seek advice from peers and teachers look for those in the same position as you or those who have already done what you're trying to, do ask them about their process and see how yours measures up you might find things that they do or have done, that you would like to adopt into your process read books about people you admire try to find details about their process that you can incorporate into your own lastly do challenging things, to even have a chance of fostering **the growth mindset** you have to step outside of your comfort zone people, who don't leave their comfort zone begin to believe that their success is due to innate talent. because everything comes so easy to them for, example, a student who is never challenged in school will begin to believe that they're innately smart I get a's, therefore, I'm smart they might say the result comes so easy to them that they don't even think about the process.

unfortunately, all I see is the result and they get attached to that when they inevitably get a bad grade they'll think that they're dumb they lose faith in themselves,

because, they didn't get the result that they're used to receiving so easily.

on the other hand, going outside of your comfort zone forces you to adopt **the growth mindset** to avoid :

shattering under the weight of adversity you have to focus on and adjust the process, because you can't possibly achieve the result you desire with your current process, by definition that's what it means to step outside of your comfort zone. so now you know about **the growth mindset** why it's important and some ideas on how to develop it keep
in mind that it takes a lot of effort todevelop and that'll always be a battle to avoid falling into **the fixed mindset**

people will say certain things or things will happen that trigger a fixed mindset in us it's important to notice when this is happening and try to avoid getting fixed in place
I'd like to close out with this quote from Carol Dweck:

"the path to a growth mindset is a lifelong journey, not a proclamation"

I Hope You Like This Mini Book About The Perfect Mindset for Success

Leaders Notebook

Leaders Notebook

www.ingramcontent.com/pod-product-compliance
Lightning Source LLC
Chambersburg PA
CBHW070915220526
45466CB00005B/2218